Food Fuel

Dr. Ranj Singh

Illustrated by David Semple

Houghton Mifflin Harcourt.

Food Fuel was originally published in English in 2016.
This edition is published by arrangement with Oxford University Press.

U.S. Edition copyright © 2019 by Houghton Mifflin Harcourt Publishing Company
Text and illustrations © Oxford University Press 2016

All rights reserved. No part of this work may be reproduced or transmitted in any form or by any means, electronic or mechanical, including photocopying or recording, or by any information storage or retrieval system, without the prior written permission of the original copyright owner identified herein, unless such copying is expressly permitted by federal copyright law.

Printed in China

ISBN 978-0-358-26292-3

1 2 3 4 5 6 7 8 9 10   XXXX   28 27 26 25 24 23 22 21 20 19

4500000000   A B C D E F G

Acknowledgments
Series Editor: Greg Foot

Cover and inside illustrations by David Semple

Houghton Mifflin Harcourt Publishing Company
125 High Street
Boston, MA 02110
www.hmhco.com

Contents

Brilliant Bodies 4

Food, Glorious Food! 6

Who Ate All the Carbohydrates? 8

Lean, Mean, Protein! 10

Fat? I'll Have Some of That! 12

Sprinkles of Vitamins and Minerals 14

Wonderful Water 16

Follow the Journey of Food 18

What's on Your Plate? 20

Glossary 22

Index 23

Brilliant Bodies

The human body is brilliant. It's better than any machine because it can think, move, and grow!

Your brilliant body is always busy, even when you're asleep. In just 24 hours you will take over 25,000 breaths!

Just like a car needs gas or electricity, your body needs fuel to keep it going. This fuel helps your body do all the different things that it has to do. It also stops you from getting ill.

You just need to make sure you put the right kind of fuel into your body.

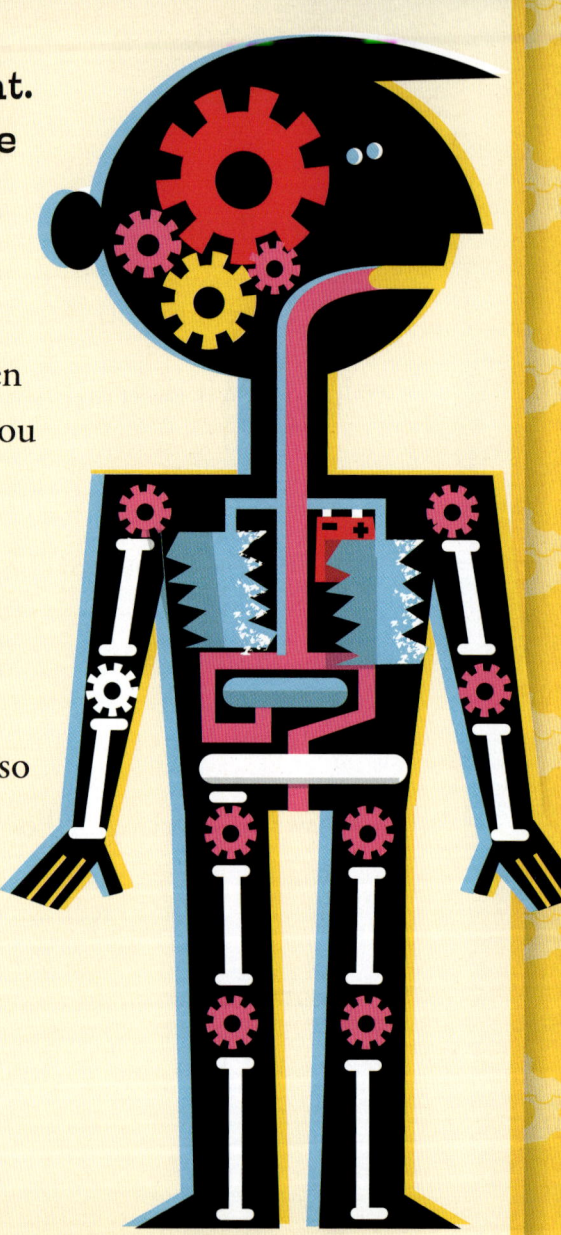

That special fuel isn't gas or electricity... it's food!

I'm Dr. Ranj. Together, we're going to learn about what fuel your body needs and why. Let's go!

Food, Glorious Food!

There are many different types of food, like fruit, vegetables, meat, fish, bread, and so much more! All of the food we eat is made up of lots of little things which our bodies need.

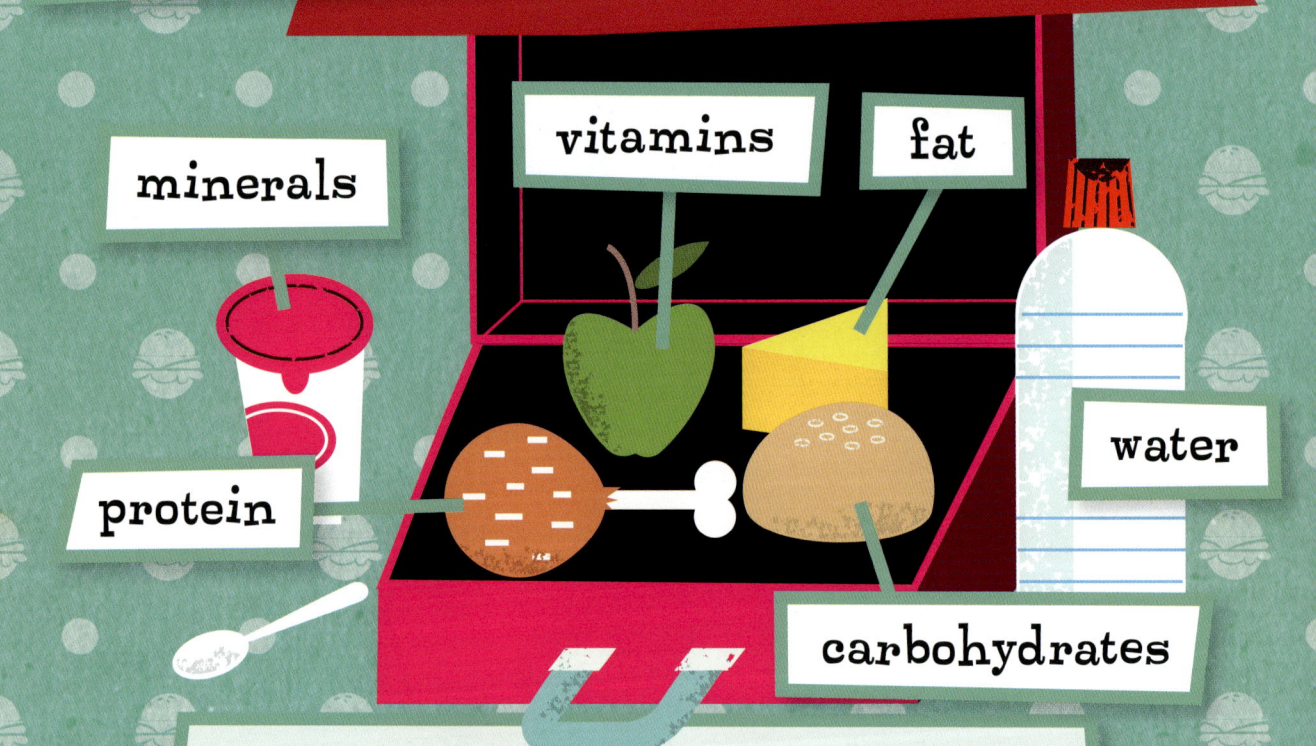

minerals

vitamins

fat

protein

water

carbohydrates

Each of these things does a very important job inside your body. They are in everything we eat.

Some of these things give us **energy**...

...and some of them help our bodies work.

Now take a look at this food fuel meter. When we eat all the right things, our fuel meter is full and we have everything that we need.

As you read on, keep an eye on the fuel meter. This will show you how much food fuel each of the different things gives you!

Who Ate All the Carbohydrates?

Carbohydrates (say kar-boe-high-drates) are our main source of energy. They are important because they give us most of the fuel we need every day.

Foods that have lots of carbohydrates in them include:

SIMPLE CARBOHYDRATES	COMPLEX CARBOHYDRATES
sugar	rice
cake	potatoes
cookies	bread

There are two different kinds of carbohydrates: simple and complex. Simple carbohydrates give us a quick boost of energy. Usually this only lasts for a short time. Complex carbohydrates release energy much more slowly, and so they last longer. It's a bit like the story of the hare and the tortoise.

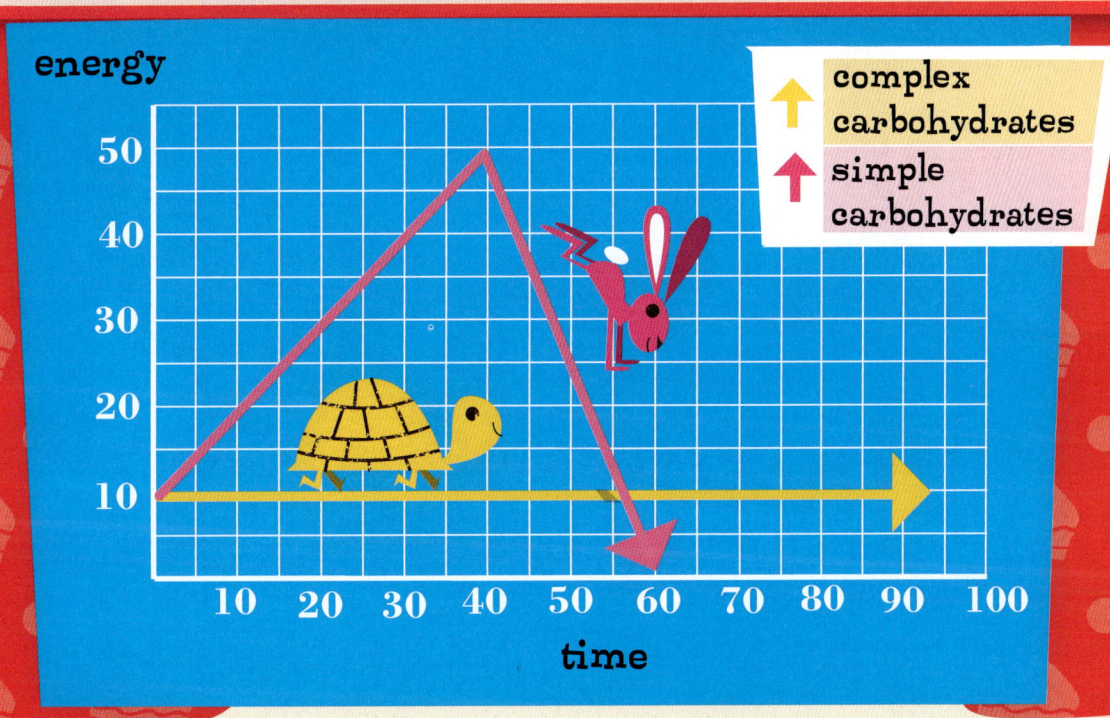

energy

50
40
30
20
10

↑ complex carbohydrates
↑ simple carbohydrates

10 20 30 40 50 60 70 80 90 100
time

Beware! Too many carbohydrates aren't good. It might give us more energy than we need. Unless we use that extra energy up, our bodies will store it as **fat**.

Too much sugar (found in simple carbohydrates) can also be bad for your teeth!

Lean, Mean Protein!

Protein (say proh-teen) is everywhere inside your body.

Most of the protein in your body is in your muscles, and it is in everything from your hair right down to your toenails. You also need protein to grow.

Without protein, our bodies would become a big mushy mess!

Our bodies get protein from lots of different foods. Some proteins come from animals.

Some people don't eat these, so luckily we can get protein from other foods, too.

Your body can also use protein for energy. That's important if it doesn't get enough energy from other food sources.

It's also why your muscles shrink if you don't eat properly!

Fat? I'll Have Some of That!

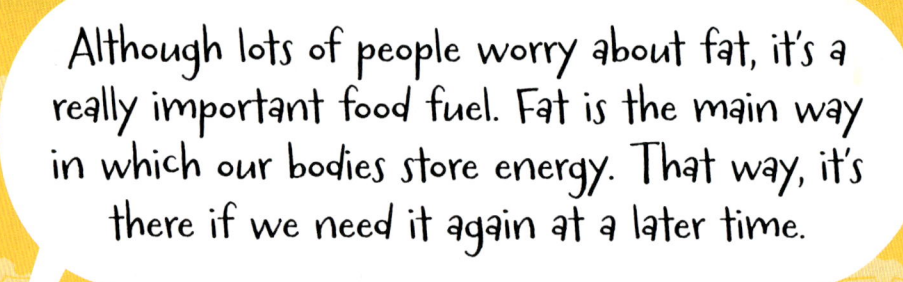

"Although lots of people worry about fat, it's a really important food fuel. Fat is the main way in which our bodies store energy. That way, it's there if we need it again at a later time."

Our bodies can get the fat we need from foods like these:

butter

cream

However, we don't need very much of it. If too much fat gets stored, it can make us unhealthy.

Fat has lots of other useful jobs inside the body too.

It's an important ingredient in our brains.

It helps our bodies to get **vitamins** from food.

It helps us to stay warm.

Whales and seals have fat under their skin called "blubber." It stores energy and keeps them warm!

Sprinkles of Vitamins and Minerals

Our brilliant bodies need a bit of help to do all the things they do.

Vitamins and **minerals** are like tiny little helpers.

Vitamins and minerals help our bodies to . . .

- grow,
- get energy from food,
- keep working in top condition,
- heal and repair themselves.

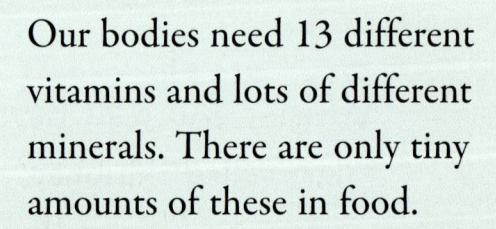

Our bodies need 13 different vitamins and lots of different minerals. There are only tiny amounts of these in food.

Luckily we only need very small amounts, so a good diet should give you enough!

How many of these do you know?

VITAMINS

Spinach – vitamin A
Meat – vitamin B
Orange – vitamin C
Fish – vitamin D
Nuts – vitamin E

MINERALS

Salt – sodium
Milk – calcium
Green vegetables – iron
Bananas – potassium
Mushrooms – zinc

Wonderful Water

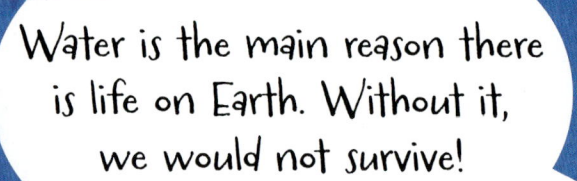

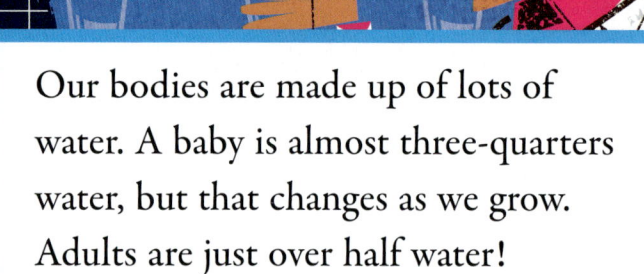

Water is the main reason there is life on Earth. Without it, we would not survive!

Our bodies are made up of lots of water. A baby is almost three-quarters water, but that changes as we grow. Adults are just over half water!

50%
75%

If you took all the water out, you would shrivel up like a raisin!

Water is used in everything that our bodies do. That's why we need to drink plenty of it. We can get water from the food we eat and from lots of different drinks.

Our **kidneys** are really good at getting rid of any extra water we don't need. They also use water to remove some of the waste that our bodies make.

It all comes out when you go to the bathroom!

Follow the Journey of Food

When we put food into our mouths, it starts a long journey through the **digestive system**. It can take a couple of days for food to travel from the beginning to the end!

1. Mouth
Food gets chewed up into little pieces and mixed with saliva (spit).

2. Esophagus
Swallow! Food goes down the **esophagus** into the **stomach**.

3. Stomach
Food gets mixed up with acid and broken down into mushy stuff.

4. Intestines, liver, and pancreas

The mushy stuff goes into the **intestines**. This is where the body takes out all the special things it needs, with the help of the **liver** and the **pancreas**.

5. Kidneys

Any extra water and some waste from the body is taken out by the kidneys.

6. Rectum

Anything left in the intestines that the body doesn't need comes out from the **rectum** when you go to the bathroom.

An adult's digestive system is around 33 feet long!

What's on Your Plate?

So, to keep our food fuel meters full, we need to have enough of all the different things we have learned about. This is what we call a balanced diet. It contains all of the different things we need in the right amounts.

vitamins and minerals

protein

fat

water

carbohydrates

Depending on where you are from, you might eat different things. But you still need to make sure your diet is balanced.

Eating well is important to stay healthy. Now you know how to keep your fuel meter full so your brilliant body can work at its best! See you next time!

Glossary

carbohydrates: the main source of energy for the human body – it makes up most of the food we eat

digestive system: the part of the body that food travels through after we eat or drink it

energy: produced from food fuel and needed to do things like walk, run, and play

esophagus: the food pipe that carries food from the mouth to the stomach when we swallow

fat: a really good source of energy, but any energy the body does not need right away is stored

intestines: the part of the body where food goes after it has left the stomach

kidneys: the part of the body that gets rid of extra water and some waste

liver: a part of the body that helps us to take the things we need from food

minerals: found in small amounts in food and have many different jobs inside the body

pancreas: a part of the body that helps us to take the things we need from food

protein: used as a building block for everything in the human body and is important for growth

rectum: the end of the intestines – any waste from the intestines comes out of here

stomach: the part of the body that mixes food with acid – this helps to break it down into mushy stuff

vitamins: found in small amounts in food and have lots of different jobs inside the body

Index

balanced diet	20–21
carbohydrates	8–9
digestive system	18–19
esophagus	18
fat	9, 12–13
intestines	18
kidneys	17, 19
liver	18
minerals	14–15
pancreas	18
protein	10–11
rectum	19
saliva	18
sugar	8–9
water	16–17
vitamins	13, 14–15

About the Author

I'm a children's doctor and also a TV presenter. I live in London and work there in a children's hospital. When I'm not at the hospital, I travel all over the country making TV programs for children and grown-ups.

When I was growing up, I wanted to become an astronaut, and then a teacher, and then I decided to become a doctor. I find my job really fun, and love helping people feel better. When I'm not working, I listen to music, dance, and eat all kinds of interesting food!